HAL•LEONARD®

VIOLIN
PLAY-ALONG

AUDIO
ACCESS
INCLUDED

Taylor Davis

PLAYBACK+
Speed • Pitch • Balance • Loop

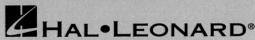

To access audio visit:
www.halleonard.com/mylibrary
Enter Code
7771-2226-9570-3183

Cover photo by Aga Jones Photography

Jerry Loughney, violin
Audio arrangements by Dan Maske
Recorded and Produced by Dan Maske

ISBN 978-1-4950-7105-8

HAL•LEONARD®
7777 W. BLUEMOUND RD. P.O. BOX 13819 MILWAUKEE, WI 53213

Visit Hal Leonard Online at
www.halleonard.com

Colors of the Wind

from POCAHONTAS
Music by Alan Menken
Lyrics by Stephen Schwartz
Arranged by Taylor Davis

Dearly Beloved

from KINGDOM HEARTS

Music by Yoko Shimomura
Arranged by Taylor Davis

Sadness and Sorrow

from the television series NARUTO
By Purojekuto Musashi
Arranged by Taylor Davis

Dragonborn
(Skyrim Theme)

By Jeremy Soule
Arranged by Taylor Davis

Fairy Tail

from the television series FAIRY TAIL
By Yashuharu Takanashi
Arranged by Taylor Davis and Lara de Wit

Game of Thrones

Theme from the HBO Series GAME OF THRONES

By Ramin Djawadi
Arranged by Taylor Davis

He's a Pirate

from PIRATES OF THE CARIBBEAN: THE CURSE OF THE BLACK PEARL

Music by Klaus Badelt, Geoffrey Zanelli and Hans Zimmer
Arranged by Taylor Davis and Adam Gubman

Last of the Mohicans

(Main Theme)

from the Twentieth Century Fox Motion Picture THE LAST OF THE MOHICANS

By Trevor Jones
Arranged by Taylor Davis